When Men Cry:
Life's Later Voyages

poems by
Neil H. Spirtas

Writings herein are the product of Neil H. Spirtas, and he is responsible for the contents. Wider Perspectives Publishing reserves 1st run rights of this work and all rights revert to the author upon delivery. Author then reserves the right to grant or restrict reprinting of this volume in whole or in part and may resubmit for contests and anthologies at will. Reproduction of the contents of this volume, in whole or in part, is only permissible with consent of the author.

Acknowledged

Heartfelt gratitude to the journal editors in which the below poems appeared previously. Some of them are in a slightly different format:
FreeXpresSions for "How Men Cry", "Isn't Dying Twice
    Enough?" & "Crying May Distort Men's Looks"
The Eclectic Muse: A Poetry Journal for "That Day", "How Men
    Cry" & "Isn't Dying Twice Enough?"

My deepest gratitude goes to Wider Perspectives Publishing in Hampton Roads, Virginia. James Wilson believed in my work and gave it life.

I would like to thank the following people for their guidance, encouragement, and love in the development of these poems;

To my mentors: Clara Macri, M.B. McLatchey, Herbie Rose, Ben Hyland, Gianna Russo, Dr. C. David Anderson, Dr. Mark Clark, Pete Carlson, Graciela Giles, Tom Moseley and Jo Ann Cote.

To my English teacher Mrs. Pittman from Belleville Township High School West. When I was a junior, she told me I had the talent to be a professional writer.

To my fellow Manatee Chamber of Commerce colleagues, members, and closest friends, particularly my faithful assistant for 15 years, Lisa Reeder, who stimulated my writing and without whom there would be no poetry.

To my loving mother and father and dearest wife, Robyn – always at my side – encouraging me to learn, write, and reach my goal.

Published by Wider Perspectives Publishing,
Hampton Roads, Virginia
Copyright Neil H. Spirtas November 2019
1st ed.ISBN: 9781700359247   2nd ed. ISBN: **978-1-952773-18-1**

Foreword

Commentary on When Men Cry

In this debut poetry collection, *When Men Cry*, Neil Spirtas recalls for us what the great Romantic poets knew: that in turning to nature, we enlighten and heal ourselves. In a series of poems that celebrate the dignity of the aged – and the shadowy dignity of victims of Alzheimer's disease – Spirtas turns to the natural world to ignite his imagination and to find the tools of a medic for his poems' subjects.

"His neighbors brought him home," we are told in a verse line so simple and direct, our hearts ache for not only for the subject suffering from Alzheimer's, but for his family and friends – *and his neighbors*. And yet, the poems do not loiter in loss. In a poem titled "Happiness Is…" – as in so many of the poems in this collection – Spirtas casts his theme of the ravages of growing old against a natural-world tableau that at once corrects our understanding of old age and redeems us. When diseases accompanying age can so disorient us and uproot us, nature reminds us of roots as anchors.

> Roots not wobbly from torrential rains,
> Anchors like stoic live oaks.

To the extent that these poems seem to converse with nature, one is reminded again and again of Wordsworth's "The Fountain: A Conversation". In Wordsworth's poem, the speaker in his innocent youth converses with his seventy-two-year-old friend, Matthew, and reflects on the unfortunate changes that accompany experience and age. In Wordsworth's poem, as in Spirtas' collection, aging, challenging experiences, and suffering are all as natural an event as the earthly setting we have been delivered into.

In their craft and tenderness, these poems recommend courage and resilience where most would find despair. "Canst thou minister to a mind diseased?" Shakespeare's Macbeth asks. Spirtas' <u>When Men Cry</u> answers with a resounding *Yes*.

      – M.B. McLatchey – widely published poet, recipient of 2013 May Swenson Poetry Award for *The Lame God,* Florida Poet Laureate for Volusia County, Assoc. Professor of Classics Embry-Riddle Aeronautical University.

Introduction

This book is personally offered on behalf of my beloved Aunt Judy, Uncle Mark, cousin Stan and dear friend, artist Herbie Rose. Both (my aunt and Herbie) had been afflicted with and institutionalized due to Alzheimer's disease. Herbie passed away in 2017. My Uncle Mark gave me the determination to write because of his own courageous, humorous yet tender blogging on his condition. Keeping one's sense of humor, Uncle Mark reminds me, helps to keep one plugging along. Mark and my cousin Stan both have Parkinson's – a degenerative disorderof the central nervous system. Additionally, this book is presented in tribute to those tens of millions worldwide suffering from Alzheimer's and to their caregivers.

– Neil H. Spirtas

Dedicated

Since the writing and publishing of this Chapbook, dear friend and artist Herbie Rose passed away. May this book help loved ones and friends cope with a loss, remembering their spirit, and expressing their love and affections while in this world.

A special note of recognition to one of the greatest orators of all time, Cicero, who said, "The Glory of Old Age is Influence" and to renown poet William Shakespeare who wrote, "Give sorrow words as the grief that does not speak knits up the overwrought heart and bids it break."

Contents

That Day	2
The Manatee River	4
Is this Happiness?	6
When Men Cry	8
Crying Too Long	10
Isn't Dying Twice Enough?	12
What is Best?	14
Love Inspires	16
Color Beautifies Time	18
E Pluribus Unum	20
Aging	22
Getting Out of Your Own Skin	24
On Old Age	26
The Coming of Cataracts: Starting All Over Again	28
Forgive - Forget Not; Mnemosyne and Poppy-Laden Fields	30
In Life … In Death	32
Retired or Refocused?	34
Is There a Life Lesson I Am Missing?	36
Go to Sleep	38
Hear Our Plea	40

That Day ...

His neighbors brought him home.
That day Herbie left us battling Alzheimer's,
his immortality had already begun.
That day he became another statistic among the five million,
his days numbered.
That day after he walked alone through his Village,
he became lost.
That day he no longer extended his art to others or himself,
his life dramatically changed forever.
That day when those whom loved him for his triumphs,
his disaster they now feared for.
That day ...

*God grant me the Senility to forget the people I never liked anyway;
the good fortune to run into the ones I do;
and the eyesight to tell the difference.*
The Senility Prayer

– Ben Witherington

The Manatee River

Life's changed on the river.
Nothing so beautiful than to be
on the majestic Manatee.
With porpoises airborne and snook galore,
based on local lore.

Spanish origin claims its mouth,
according to history.
But no one owns it,
clones it,
controls its fury.
A river that flows with the sea
and the inland waters,
whose natural bounty fulfills loftier quarters.

Upon whose waves ebb and crest,
she giveth and taketh away among the best.
Poems written by fools like me;
watercolors painted by Herbie,
only Nature can make the Manatee.

Is this Happiness?

A sunny, splendid day,
Florida in the rainy season turns cloudy,
Nature's garden-fresh smell trails the rain,
then precipitously, sprinkles cold.
Dreams real upon the morning dew,
potentials well within reach of the pearly gates.
Roots not wobbly from torrential rains,
anchors like stoic live oaks.

Gained over night or endured,
in the exclusivity of your twilight years?
A lump sum, cash or credit,
Is this the happiness you wanted to get?

Nicomachean Ethics aside,
a comfortable state of mind.
Lucky, joyful,
and living well.
Giving, but not to tell.
Regrets few …
then whom of you,
are happy?

When Men Cry

Men cry in utter stillness
behind closed doors.
Men inherently restrain,
men woefully whimper
when they're ill.

Admired for mighty chests and
broad shoulders,
fathers teach sons
to master their emotions.
Be independent,
deficient of weakness.

So, others -
can easily lean on,
can confidently cry on,
can profoundly depend on,
their deeply-rooted trunks;
their eagle-spanned wings.

Crying Too Long …

At the most inopportune time -
when the tide
may be turning,
when bearing misfortune
may be best without crying,
when often in vain.

Men wearing kotinos,
keeping the blinding sun shining,
retaining the relentless rain from getting in.
Building indoor comfort –
controlled domes to enable
Olympic Games to play.
Men's egos escalate
with sports enthusiasm;
psyches soar with Machiavellianism.
Why cry to their wit's end?
Does it help Atlas' to ascend?
Or, bow to their brazen knees?

Crying may distort men's looks,
beware what parents
prophetically say,
delicately refrain;
cry too long and your face …
will stay that way.

Isn't Dying Twice Enough?

Artists no longer able to grip their brush.
Great communicators' verbal talents diminish.
Struggling with their sentences and paragraphs,
dangling to be read in mid-air.

Peering into their subconscious souls,
into their eyes and their deep pools,
where the murky ponds bottom
cannot be seen.

Where their words
escape into a fine mist,
lost forever upon the sun's blinding light.
Where names and their relations
become a big blur.

Elie Wiesel says we die twice.
A second time when our names
never to be forgotten,
are said for the last time.

Where on this earth
do the names, the faces, the places go?
Millions of lives have been lost already,
in this stream of forgetful oblivion.

Isn't dying twice enough?

Blessed are the forgetful, for they get the better even of their blunders

– Friedrich Nietzsche

What is Best?

What is life all about?
Does anyone really know?
Where can you find out?
Where are you to go?

Like a ship going out to sea,
at first on course then drifting afar from free.
Short on food, short on patience,
you lose sight of what is righteous.

You must have a full belly or become brutal,
otherwise life is hardened and futile.
These elements not of eternal importance,
they enslave you to mundane forces.

From successful trips on earlier voyages,
from proper guidance,
from God's grace, you find there is relevance.
Paint the stars, as if they steer and speak with clout;
Be brave, don't fret and find your better route.

Your greatest gift – your immortal, artful choice,
to do with life as you see fit – with your own voice.
Doesn't this warrant a constant vigil and quest?
To ask what it's all about and do what is best.

*Be not the slave of your own past – plunge into the sublime seas,
dive deep, and swim far, so you shall come back
with new self- respect, with new power, and
with an advanced experience that shall
explain and overlook the old.*
– Ralph Waldo Emerson

Love Inspires

us to shape our world
to ignite the spark in others.

Love may
not feed the hungry
nor cement a broken bone
nor save us from tsunamis
nor bring back the concentration camp victims.

But love can
help you look at yourself
reflect at the river's edge
see most clearly on a mountaintop
lead our country on the field of battle
heal a wounded soldier's sorrow
engage a heart for one's fellow human beings.

Rise higher than yourself alone.

Color Beautifies Time

Watercolors are reflective, mixed blessings,
a challenge to capture and to control.
The day's sun arises and lights up the world's reflections.

Keeper of memory - Mnemosyne's,
flowing rivers flood with light and color;
Gracefully deiced by the sun.
gradually shadows dim,
dwindling and withering away,
upon the moon's admission.

Beautiful, brilliant, hiding.
Life's last days resemble
the twilight of charcoals,
fading to dark.

Painting time is like life's accents –
avian abundance of the rainbow's arc.
Musical and elusive hues,
a tinge of greys, yellows, and blues.
Capturing their joyful, vivid, natures,
savoring the memories … not too fast.
Never a fleeting moment,
harmonious how 'color beautifies time'.

Most of the shadows of this life are caused by standing in one's own sunshine.

– Ralph Waldo Emerson

E Pluribus Unum

Out of many comes one
many gods into one
many states into one.

Coming together as one or
breaking apart as no one.

One attains more as a team
one reaches beyond to exceed their grasp.

One person's act of hatred; fans the fumes of crime against humanity
one named Adam murders 20 first-graders at Sandy Hook.

One day's supply of oil marks the eight-day Hanukah miracle
one Anne Frank shares with 30 million her powerful story.

One colony of aphids multiply to destroy rose gardens
one thousand synagogues torched in two days.

One elephant stays behind to mourn the death of a herd member
one's loving kindness can make one household of the entire human race.

Coming together as one
breaking apart as no one.

Aging

When rainbows lose their color,
when tropical storms hit landfall,
when human talents no longer shine.
God-given gifts: where are they to be found?

Squandering almost aimlessly?
Turning into a dilettante,
reverting to childhood or
soaring into an enriching, timeless corridor?

Aging can immerse daylight into darkness,
darkness into day,
sounds rendered into silence.
Stalks of corn decay,
unharvested they wilt,
then wither away,
exquisite flowers eventually turn,
colorless, odorless, unless,
savored by the brilliance of their last days.

The Sea of Galilee nourishing,
the Dead Sea springs non-reciprocating.
Can we go beyond past, mere silhouettes in a maze?
Can we gratify and sing of life's praise?
Can we survive lists of endangerments?
Eating the fruits that have sustained us,
drinking of the waters in the Days of Awe.

Old age is like a plane flying through a storm. Once you're aboard there's nothing you can do.

– Golda Meir

Getting Out of Your Own Skin

Spiritual forces were at work
for renowned artist Herbie,
he would go to places and colors
the naked eye couldn't see,
wildly creative and richly detailed.
In capturing Nature's shadows and light,
he never failed.

Being true to himself,
he would say, the artist's hand
was an expression of one's self.
His verbalizing and teaching of art
his life's journey
did not come easily.
His students declared
he taught them selflessly.

Striving to do what he knew best,
landscapes, city scenes, architectural renderings –
above all the rest.
"Get out of your own skin,"
he would say … to only mean,
look from within.

On Old Age

A Pulitzer Prize winning author took up writing at 65,
Colonel Sanders made it big in his sixties.
Previously an elderly masculine characteristic,
virility is now a physiological disorder.
Sixties are the new forties.

There is no static time,
on Old Age.
No phony retreating,
no entire retiring,
no lateral shifts in mind.

Garner the abundant fruits of your work,
Old Age's sweet reward of success.
Choose your launching pad wisely -
inspired by the winds of leadership,
heedlessly the flowers begin to fade,
imagine a learning journey.

Atlas lifting the weight off your shoulders,
drawing the curtains for the last scenes of your play,
Moses wandering the desert,
Cicero declaring the glory of Old Age is influence,
wisdom and peace coming with Old Age when,
living with honor, grace and in virtue,
retiring to the most honorable of places,
engaging in a life of your heart's desire.

Dying in a just society unabashedly unafraid,
fighting off youthful tragedy,
voyaging, as pledged, with loved ones before thee.

Ne'er alone,
peacefully,
do you go,
pen in hand at 81,
like Plato?

Be ashamed to die until you have won some victory for humanity.

– Horace Mann

The Coming of Cataracts:
Starting All Over Again

Can't change by conventions
what was meant by Nature?
How about the creeping, coming of
cataracts
and the newly found colors
from this life-science cycle
that cracks colorblindness?

Ocular inserts and surgery
correct many an eyesight
going back forty years or more for me
when some of life's most vivid hues
were bright and bold and beautiful
beyond the now dim,
discolored, drab of old age.

The wise use of laser conventions
of cataract measures take minutes
before sights are restored once again,
lights become sparkling clear,
glasses no more to wear!

Salamanders grow new limbs once lost
caterpillars turn into butterflies
clownfish change their gender with
role reversal upon death.
Giant Trivali fish snag birds out of
midair,
Pacific salmon spawn,
then the life cycle is
starting all over again.

Forgive - Forget Not;
Mnemosyne and Poppy-Laden Fields

From taking your medicinal fill
of forgetting,
of unforgiving,
of tightening the circle
from one's being,
upon entering the Myth of Er.

Forgive oneself ...
to elevate one's soul,
where guilt will be purged,
where judgments journey, but not,
where Mnemosyne's river of forgetfulness flows.

Forgive and unleash the
misdirected Karma that hardens grudges;
comparable to swallowing cyanide -
to harm others,
to indulging beyond consumption -
to reverse pain and disease.

Forget not the cancers of anger ...
where wrongdoers and resentment remain,
where injustices infest,
where shattered dreams sour.

Banish future greater harm,
akin to fine thoroughbreds
marked for life on their shins and hoofs,
marked by the greatest of wrongdoings,
marked unforgiven but not unforgotten.

Go beyond the emotional pangs and
mortal displays of ruthless revenge,
to helping friends,
to not harming enemies,
to climbing new heights of contemplation.

Forget not the fragrant smell of a rose,
the freshness of fallen rain,
the fertile aroma of the orange blossom,
the sweet-smell of lavender and poppy-laden fields.

In Life … In Death

Death for many is an unknown
closure of doors and a private opening with views,
as sundry as the clouds in the sky and
as earthy as the soils below,
where the great philosophers philosophize,
the prophets prophesize and
the poets are in prose.

Keen as the eye can see and the mind can contemplate,
eternal hope brings belief and humility in life.
Good deeds and contrition,
render destiny from one's dreams in death.

Repentance for repentance-sake and
a rewarding "free ticket" to Heaven is flawed.
The means of a good or failed life does not separate from
the end result in the hereafter.

Today, just men and women wrongly die alone,
absent the company of their friends and loved ones.
Is this not an absolute truth?
A natural act not to be feared or lamented?
Technology and modern science have all but conventionally
removed the act of violence in death,
to bring about more peace and comfort in life.
Unabashedly, in life we exalt,
in death, we fear and shun.

Man, alone cannot create man,
nor know death or to defy biological certainty.
nonetheless … to endeavor,
to contemplate life's purpose,
to visualize beyond the grave.

Every 67 seconds someone in America develops Alzheimer's.

– Bright Focus Foundation

Retired or Refocused?

Friends glimpse into their future
curiously wondering what it is like.
Time appears abundant,
traveling as fast as the days are long.
Nonetheless, slipping away,
as quick as sand in the hourglass.

Choice hath become a freedom lost
for so many … for so many years.
Obliviousness around the street corner,
for those caught unawares.

Alarm clocks no longer
an absolute bedside fixture.
True friends return your call,
others already forgotten your name.
Once esteemed, now a stranger.

Why didn't you retire earlier?
Why did you retire in the first place?
you ask yourself,
Why do the hummingbirds head southward for thousands of miles?
to only turn around northward,
to do it all over again.

Old friends have a precious renewed taste,
liken to a favorite fine wine.
Life is defined by whom you are,
rather than the nametag you wear.
"Retired" connotes prior tiredness -
discharged, old aged,
or are you refocused and revived?

Go forward not awkwardly,
sheepishly, in reverse.
Move candidly toward your dreams.
laid out not to pasture –
in the northeast forty with the farm animals.
Gather in the greying owl's piercing vantage point,
dwell not in demolished rain forests.
Choose a refocused status nestled in the future,
built on the diverging branches of the past.

Is There a Life Lesson I Am Missing?

Clouds drifting,
into skies of sapphire,
white lights and star sights,
of which we never tire.

Airy faces and figures transpire,
to whit we aspire.
A rare Moon's eclipse,
upon the heavenly bodies' lips.

All the whilst … Nature's bounties go to waste yet stay,
when the forests whither into fire-breeding decay,
when the majestic vistas go disregarded,
when the greatest of artists' works are concluded,
when parents and relatives no longer have much say.

Is there a life lesson
I am missing about this tragedy?
Drawing us toward reality,
challenging us at every turn,
is this what we are to learn?

Go to Sleep

While going to rest tonight,
wanting to awaken full of life,
to make the day go right,
lie down, so tomorrow you will be bright.

Oh … to dance, to sing, to draw throughout the night!

Can you envision how it illuminates the spirit?
How the eve brings on your most creative concerns,
full days short of contemplation,
they have worked us to the bone with frustration.

To be entirely content today will not suffice.

Take your rest now my uncle, dear aunt and,
old man … worry not - whilst you can.
Go to sleep, let your body unwind,
unchain the melody in your mind -
to a lighter, gentler time.

Hear Our Plea

To all fellow poets hear our plea,
for better words than Alzheimer's or lunacies.
Shunt the stereotypes and indignities aside,
allow the afflicted to cope with, to hide,
from remarks repugnant and disruptive,
akin to impairments mildly cognitive.

Don't tolerate the alive but memory - stricken,
to be stigmatized -
resembling them as children,
to be dehumanized -
imprisoning them with brain shackles, like old autos in a used car lot,
to be marginalized.

The brains 'hippocampus' region has been consumed subtlety,
twenty-first century progress overcome these many forms of senility.
Doctors, scientists, researchers hear my plea;
alleviate the sorrows surrounding my Aunt Judy,
thwart the yet-to-be renamed disease
from the annals of history.

About the Poems

"The Manatee River" – is inspired and in blessed memory of one of my mother's favorite poems *Trees*, by Sergeant Joyce Kilmer. It was revised to include my thoughts of artist and good friend Herbie Rose who painted watercolors of the Manatee River, landscapes and other water bodies in southwest Florida and his native Port Antonio, Jamaica.

"Aging" – includes the mentioning of the (ten) *Days of Awe* which refers to the solemn days between the Jewish high holidays of Rosh Hashanah (new year) and Yom Kippur (day of atonement). The overriding tone of these interim days are repentance, forgiveness and taking stock of one's life. It is a spiritual journey of introspection and symbolic observance (*Eating the fruits*) … such as apples, pomegranates, honey (*Drinking of the waters*) … in the Days of Awe.

"Go to Sleep"—is in slightly different form, originally written in first person, from when I was a young man in graduate school and first composed. The emphasis changed to an older man or woman.

Writers and correspondents that I have gleaned from their newspaper and on-line articles include Paul Jerome, *St. Petersburg Times*, very thorough, artfully written expose - "The Artist as Art", published Feb. 29, 2000; J. Nielsen, *Sarasota Herald Tribune*, Dec. 4, 2013, about Herbie Rose as founder, local hero and honorary Mayor of the Village of the Arts; Hector Ferran, *Bradenton Patch*, July 19, 2012 – "Florida Scenes with a Caribbean Flair" details a poster by Herbie Rose designed for boat builder Chris-Craft later used to promote the restoration of the Statue of Liberty and his collections used to promote his homeland of Jamaica in the Summer Games, 1992 in Barcelona, Spain, and; Frank O. Copley's translation of *Cicero's; On Old Age and On Friendship*, University of Michigan Press, Copyright 1967 for the discussions about the glory of old age, memory and retirement.

"Color Beautifies Time" – revised from an original poem recognizing my sister's anniversary and the importance and grace of time's passage.

"Forgive–Forget Not;" is motivated by Harold Kushner's *Overcoming Life's Disappointments*.

Colophon
Brought to you by Wider Perspectives Publishing, care of James Wilson, with the mission of advancing the poetry and creative community of Hampton Roads, Virginia, and beyond.
See our production of works from …

Tanya Cunningham
Gloria Darlene Mann
Terra Leigh
Ray Simmons
SA Borders-Shoemaker
Taz Waysweete'
Bobby K. (The Poor Man's Poet)
J. Scott Wilson (TEECH!)
Zach Crowe
Lisa M. Kendrick
Dezz
Symay Rhodes

Charles Wilson
Jorge Mendez & JT Williams
Sarah Eileen Williams
Stephanie Diana (Noftz)
the Hampton Roads Artistic Collective
Jason Brown (Drk Mtr)
Martina Champion
Tony Broadway
Ken Sutton
Crickyt J. Expression
Chichi Iwuorie
Cass IsFree

… and others to come soon.

We promote and support poetic artists
from the seats, from the stands,
from the snapping fingers and clapping hands
from the pages, and the stages
and now we pass them forth to the ages

Check for the above artists on FaceBook, the Virginia Poetry Online channel on YouTube, and other social media.
Hampton Roads Artistic Collective is the non-profit extension of WPP and strives to simultaneously support worthy causes and the creative artists.

www.ingramcontent.com/pod-product-compliance
Lightning Source LLC
Chambersburg PA
CBHW031218090426
42736CB00009B/964